# PINK PANTHER

# BIO

## The Legacy Of Laughter, Style, And

## Innovation

**COTTON MAX**

# PINK PANTHER BIO

# TABLE OF CONTENT

# CHAPTER 1: THE BIRTH OF THE PINK PANTHER

---

## 11. Origins of the Pink Panther Franchise

The Pink Panther film series has left an indelible effect on humor, animation, and popular culture. This popular series dates back to the early 1960s, when Hollywood was experimenting with new genres and creative orientations. The Pink Panther series, however, was born from a combination of good fortune, ability, and a desire to mix comedy with suspense.

In 1963, filmmaker Blake Edwards started working on what would become The Pink Panther, a comedy-mystery picture set in the realm of international intrigue. Inspector Jacques Clouseau, a charming but inept French investigator, was the focus of the plot, as he pursued a jewel thief. The narrative revolved on the "Pink Panther," a huge, rare diamond with a peculiar defect that resembled a panther's outline.

Interestingly, the Pink Panther picture was not originally intended to center on the figure who would become its most recognized icon—Inspector Clouseau. Instead, the Pink Panther diamond functioned as the main source of curiosity. The narrative revolved on Sir Charles Lytton, a skilled burglar who sets out to steal the diamond. Clouseau, on the other hand, quickly stole the show with his crazy antics and fumbling, but endearing, attitude.

But it wasn't simply the narrative that defined the Pink Panther series; the date and conditions of its creation also played a role in its enormous popularity. In the early 1960s, there was a rising worldwide interest in both comic espionage tales and flashy heist flicks. These genres, which combine tension, comedy, and elegance, were gaining appeal. At the same time, Edwards was pushing the boundaries of comic flair by combining slapstick, satire, and farce components, resulting in a new, current tone that would appeal to a broad audience.

The creative team also featured Peter Sellers, a comedian known for his unique, incisive, and surprising sense of humor. Sellers was most recognized for his appearances in British humor, but he was also gaining popularity in Hollywood for his ability to change into a variety of distinct personas. His humorous manner complemented Edwards' vision, and his depiction of Clouseau proved crucial to the film's success.

In an unusual twist of fate, the title The Pink Panther was assigned to the project after the film's opening titles were completed. During the credits sequence design, animator DePatie-Freleng and his creative team presented the now-iconic animated version of the Pink Panther—a sleek, playful feline creature who would become the franchise's emblem. The opening sequence, which combined animation and Henry Mancini's iconic theme song, cemented the Pink Panther as an integral component of the franchise's character. The animated Pink Panther became so famous that it started to appear in its own short films, creating a distinct personality from the original live-action movie. This would go on to become one of the most well-known cartoon characters of the 1960s and 70s.

As a result, the Pink Panther franchise grew not just as a film series, but also as a larger entertainment sensation, including animated shorts, television specials, and a long-lasting impact on pop culture.

## 1.2 The Development of the Iconic Character

While Inspector Jacques Clouseau is the most well-known character in the Pink Panther series, the development of the animated Pink Panther helped establish its public image. This animated panther became the franchise's distinctive emblem, embodying the sleek, sophisticated, and elusive attributes that would define the series going forward.

DePatie-Freleng Enterprises' famed animation team developed the animated Pink Panther, which was a stroke of brilliance. This cooperation arose out of necessity: The Pink Panther film's opening credits sequence required a distinct visual representation of the diamond's mystery and attraction. The crew, lead by Friz Freleng and Hawley Pratt, opted to develop an animated character to follow the diamond as it rolled through a series of obstacles, resulting in the first appearance of the animated Pink Panther.

The persona rapidly took on a life of its own. With its basic design—a smooth, pink-colored panther with simple lines and exaggerated, but beautiful, movements—the figure radiated refinement and humorous appeal. Despite remaining entirely mute, the animated Pink Panther conveyed a wide range of emotions via visual signals and body language. His calm manner, smooth motions, and naughty conduct made him easily identifiable and attractive to people of all ages.

The Pink Panther's animation technique was also pioneering. It was inspired by European animation methods, but it had a very American feel, with a clean, minimalist design that matched Henry Mancini's jazz-infused music. The use of music was essential to the Pink Panther's appeal, with Mancini's score being inexorably tied to the character's actions and reactions.

The Pink Panther diamond was crucial to the storyline of the original live-action picture, but as the animated Pink Panther gained popularity, its significance started to eclipse the diamond's. The cartoon figure appears in a number of short films, television specials, and even comic strips, all while preserving the franchise's trademark elegance and mischief.

While the animated character lacked Inspector Clouseau's physical comic presence, it supplemented the live-action films and helped spread Pink Panther's legacy to a larger audience, especially youngsters. In reality, the animated Pink Panther sealed the franchise's position in public culture, as his image came to represent light-hearted fun, elegance, and slapstick comedy.

## 1.3 The Roles of Blake Edwards and Peter Sellers

The relationship between director Blake Edwards and actor Peter Sellers was vital to the success of the Pink Panther series. While the animated figure of the Pink Panther became legendary in its own right, it was the human element of the story—particularly the character of Inspector Clouseau—that struck a chord with fans and propelled the series to worldwide fame.

Blake Edwards, a filmmaker noted for his flexibility and ingenuity, helped shape the tone and style of the Pink Panther movies. His background in both drama and comedy provided him with the rare ability to mix slapstick hilarity with the series' dramatic, enigmatic tone. Edwards had a knack for merging broad humor with sensitivity, resulting in a picture that was both accessible and cerebral.

Perhaps the most crucial component of Edwards' worldview was his attitude toward Clouseau. The role, performed by Peter Sellers, was originally envisioned as a more obvious comedic foil—a clumsy investigator in the style of Charlie Chaplin's Tramp or the great buffoons of silent cinema. However, under Edwards' leadership, Clouseau evolved into a more complicated character who was both frustrating and appealing.

Peter Sellers' depiction of Inspector Clouseau became one of cinema's most memorable comedy performances. Sellers, recognized for his flexibility and skill of character acting, thoroughly embraced

Clouseau's ridiculousness, transforming him into the paradigm of the loving idiot. Sellers' comedic timing was spot on, and his ability to express physical humor with elegance and wildness brought the character to life in a manner that was both amusing and touching.

Sellers also gave Clouseau a distinct sense of depth, elevating him beyond the status of caricature. Despite his obvious ineptitude, Clouseau was motivated by an unwavering self-belief, which made him both miserable and strangely appealing. This contradiction became key to the Pink Panther series' comedy, as Clouseau's complete lack of knowledge often caused him to accidentally solve puzzles and defeat crooks.

The relationship between Blake Edwards and Peter Sellers was crucial in determining the tone of the Pink Panther movie. Edwards understood how to highlight Sellers' comic abilities, enabling him to improvise and produce unpredictable moments that kept spectators interested. This dynamic would characterize the series, as the films became more focused on Clouseau's comedic exploits and less on the initial narrative concerning the Pink Panther diamond.

Sellers' depiction of Clouseau was not only important to the character's appeal, but also to the general popularity of the Pink Panther series. His portrayal nailed the spirit of the character: a guy whose ignorance and self-importance were only matched by his unwavering optimism. Clouseau would become an iconic emblem of slapstick humor and the core of the Pink Panther franchise throughout the series.

This section discusses the Pink Panther franchise's beginnings, the development of its famous character, and the roles performed by director Blake Edwards and actor Peter Sellers in developing the series. To develop this into a 10,000-word chapter, you would go further into each component, offering anecdotes, cinematic analysis, and a thorough description of the franchise's creative process. You might also include interviews, behind-the-scenes anecdotes, and in-depth character studies of Clouseau and the cartoon Pink Panther..

# CHAPTER 2: THE PINK PANTHER FILMS: A CINEMATIC LEGACY

## 21. Overview of the Original Series.

The Pink Panther franchise, which began with a series of films in 1963, has become one of Hollywood's most famous and lasting cinematic legacies. Originally conceived as a comedy mystery heist film, the series expanded to encompass multiple sequels, spinoffs, animated specials, and a cultural movement. The original series, which ran from 1963 to 1978, was distinguished by its unique combination of slapstick humor, physical comedy, and smart, sometimes cerebral writing.

Blake Edwards wrote and directed the first picture, The Pink Panther (1963). It introduced the main characters who will shape the story for years to come. The narrative focuses on the worldwide intrigue surrounding the theft of the famous "Pink Panther" diamond, with Inspector Jacques Clouseau (Peter Sellers) at the heart of it all. Despite his obvious ineptitude, Clouseau becomes the story's key character, unwittingly defeating the criminal genius responsible for the crime. The film establishes the series' tone by combining a sophisticated robbery tale with slapstick humor.

The popularity of the picture led to the creation of numerous sequels, including A Shot in the Dark (1964), The Pink Panther Strikes Again (1976), and Revenge of the Pink Panther (1978), all of which featured Sellers' comic brilliance as the clumsy detective Clouseau. What distinguished these films was not just their humorous worth, but also their deft blend of mystery, suspense, and physical comedy.

In addition to Sellers' iconic performance, the pictures benefitted from a polished, attractive look. Blake Edwards was noted for his attention to detail and sense of style, which was evident in the production design and visual tone of the Pink Panther movie. The films were set in a milieu of international intrigue, exotic locales, and colorful characters, all of which contributed to their wide popularity.

The original series was built around the hilarious talent of Peter Sellers, who, under Edwards' direction, brought Inspector Clouseau to life. While Clouseau was presented as a bumbling idiot, his ludicrous actions, mixed with Sellers' superb timing and slapstick physical humor, cemented him as one of the most renowned characters in film history.

The popularity of the films was due not just to the characters' slapstick comedy, but also to the subtle complexity of the plot. The films maintained an air of refinement, owing partly to the depiction of beautiful European locations and high society settings in which most of the action took place. This was an unusual mix, but it gave the Pink Panther pictures their individual personality and enabled them to transcend the normal comedy genre.

## 2.2 The Evolution of Films

The Pink Panther flicks have evolved via both the humorous stylings of Peter Sellers' Clouseau and the series' extension into new areas. While the first films, beginning with The Pink Panther (1963), were popular in their blend of mystery and humor, the series eventually evolved into new forms, notably in narrative, characters, and general tone.

Peter Sellers' Era: Classic Comedy

The original Pink Panther films, which comprise The Pink Panther (1963), A Shot in the Dark (1964), The Pink Panther Strikes Again (1976), and Revenge of the Pink Panther (1978), are typically regarded the "golden age" of the series. These flicks laid the groundwork for the series, highlighting Sellers' comic genius in his depiction of the eternally bumbling Inspector Clouseau.

In A Shot in the Dark (1964), the emphasis moved from the robbery narrative to a murder investigation, with Clouseau, now the lead investigator on the case, once again demonstrating his powers as an unlikely hero. This episode brought the series to a new level of insanity, with Clouseau's crude but curiously effective tactics serving as the film's core of comedy.

By the time The Pink Panther Strikes Again (1976) and Revenge of the Pink Panther (1978) came out, the series had completely embraced its comedic element. Clouseau was less of a detective and more of a comedic figure—a guy who continually failed his way to success. The stories become more bizarre, such as in The Pink Panther Strikes Again, in which Clouseau must deal with a multinational conspiracy and a maniacal adversary intent on killing him.

However, the untimely death of Peter Sellers in 1980 left the Pink Panther franchise in limbo. The loss of the franchise's key protagonist created a significant obstacle to the series' future, and for a while, it seemed that the films might come to an end. Nonetheless, Edwards and the producers looked for a way to go on, and Curse of the Pink Panther was released in 1983.

The Post-Seller Era: New Faces and New Directions

After Peter Sellers' death, the Pink Panther series had the problem of continuing without its main comic force. The character of Clouseau was, of course, vital to the series, thus it was decided to choose a fresh actor to play the famed inspector. Ted Wass portrayed a new Clouseau in Curse of the Pink Panther (1983), which received lackluster reviews. The loss of Sellers' peculiar humorous approach reduced the franchise's appeal, and the picture was widely regarded as an inferior edition.

In an effort to reinvigorate the series, Son of the Pink Panther (1993) featured Roberto Benigni as Clouseau's son, Jacques Clouseau. However, like its predecessor, this picture was badly regarded, and it effectively ended the original Pink Panther film series for good.

The 2000s Reboot: A New Beginning.

After a lengthy break, the Pink Panther series returned to the big screen with the 2006 revival, The Pink Panther. Shawn Levy directed the picture, which featured Steve Martin as the new Inspector Clouseau. Martin's interpretation of the role was more obviously wacky than Sellers', with a focus on physical humor and a more general comic approach. While the revival received mixed reviews, it was successful enough at the box office to warrant a sequel, The Pink Panther 2 (2009), which again stars Steve Martin. However, the new direction lacked the same appeal of the original flicks. Despite its efforts to reintroduce Clouseau to a new audience, the franchise failed to match the original series' enchantment.

## 2.3 The Iconic Soundtrack of Henry Mancini

The Pink Panther series is defined by its iconic musical soundtrack, which was written by Henry Mancini. The music in the Pink Panther flicks became as legendary as the characters, adding to the films' allure and popularity. The main theme, with its smooth jazz rhythms and lighthearted melody, immediately became associated with the series and is now one of the most memorable pieces of cinema music in history.

Blake Edwards and Henry Mancini collaborated serendipitously to create the Pink Panther theme. Edwards, who had previously collaborated with Mancini on many projects, was seeking for a musical composition that was both smart and amusing, in keeping with the film's mix of tension and comedy. Mancini's piece, which combined jazz and symphonic elements, was an ideal match. It caught the spirit of the Pink Panther character: beautiful, naughty, and a touch cheeky.

The opening title sequence, which featured an animated Pink Panther figure cavorting to Mancini's theme, became legendary in and of itself. The fun, fluid tune was ideal for the animated panther's sneaky moves, and its marriage with the animation solidified its connection to the Pink Panther series.

Mancini's contribution on the Pink Panther movie extended beyond the theme tune. His compositions for A Shot in the Dark and its sequels brought levels of intricacy to the films, combining jazz and symphonic music to create a sophisticated and tense mood. Mancini's skilled orchestration and ability to generate mood via music elevated the pictures' humor and tension, making Pink Panther both a visual and audio experience.

Pink Panther's soundtrack became so connected with the flicks that it transcended the series, appearing in other adaptations and even finding its way into pop culture. Numerous musicians have covered the main theme, and its characteristic melody may be heard in innumerable advertisements, television programs, and parodies. Aside from the main theme, Mancini's compositions helped establish the series' general style and tone, giving the humor a feeling of elegance and mystery. In doing so, the music aided not just the comic mood but also the overall identity of the Pink Panther series. Pink Panther's soundtrack is one of the most iconic and impactful in cinematic history.

# CHAPTER 3: THE CHARACTERS

# BEHIND THE PANTHER

## 3.1 Inspector Clouseau: A Comedy Icon.

Inspector Jacques Clouseau, played by Peter Sellers, is the heart and soul of the Pink Panther films and one of the most memorable characters in movie history. His comic legacy, which combined slapstick humor, excellent timing, and unwavering self-belief, made him a crowd favorite and left an unforgettable effect on the genre of physical comedy.

### The Birth of Clouseau

The character of Clouseau was created by director Blake Edwards and writer Maurice Richlin. When creating the role of the French investigator, Edwards had a certain idea in mind: he wanted someone who embodied the ridiculousness of human nature, with his biggest defect being a total lack of self-awareness. Enter Inspector Clouseau, a well-intentioned but clumsy investigator who continually fails to solve complicated crimes due to a combination of overconfidence and clumsiness.

The part was originally planned as a supporting character in the 1963 film The Pink Panther, which followed the robbery of the legendary "Pink Panther" diamond. However, it rapidly became apparent that Clouseau was the film's genuine star. Sellers' depiction of Clouseau established the character as a lasting humorous personality, and the remainder of the series revolved around his antics.

**Clouseau's Comedy Genius**

Clouseau's steadfastness distinguishes him as a noteworthy character. Despite his many mistakes—his inability to handle even the most basic of problems, his uncomfortable dealings with others, and his unwillingness to see his own flaws—Clouseau maintains his dignity. His fake French accent, exquisite attire, and conviction in his own greatness despite overwhelming evidence to the contrary add to his hilarious appeal. Sellers' skill was in portraying Clouseau as a guy who, in his own perspective, could do no wrong, even while the world around him devolved into chaos.

Clouseau's comedy is based on the heritage of physical humor. He often slips, crashes, and fumbles his way through problems, yet he does it with utmost seriousness. It's the contrast between his crazy conduct and calm manner that makes him so entertaining. Clouseau is a fool, but the hilarity comes from the fact that he is unaware of his own idiocy. This seriousness permits Clouseau to continue his investigative job despite his many failures, and it is what makes him such a memorable character in the world of humor.

## Clouseau's Appealing Quality

While Clouseau is sometimes portrayed as a clown, his persona has an underlying sweetness that endears him to fans. Sellers gave the role a sense of innocence and sensitivity that transcended his comedic nature. He is, after all, a good-hearted guy who really wants to succeed, but his frequent misfortunes make this impossible. His unshakeable trust in his skills and unrelenting optimism, regardless of the circumstances, result in a figure that is both sad and humorous. Viewers can't help but cheer for Clouseau, even as they see him wreck everything in his way.

His interactions with other characters emphasize this fragility. Clouseau's interactions, whether he is having ludicrous disagreements with his boss, Chief Inspector Dreyfus, or clumsily flirting with his secretary, Marie, usually have an inadvertently humorous tone. His earnest desire to do the right thing, despite his incompetence, makes him a lasting comedic icon.

Clouseau's reputation as a comedic legend extends well beyond the Pink Panther series. His influence can be observed in innumerable other films and television series, and his impact on the world of humor continues to this day. Clouseau's impact can be seen everywhere, from slapstick performers like Jim Carrey to characters in animated comedies like The Simpsons. He established the stereotype of the clumsy, loving idiot who could fail in every manner possible while yet endearing himself to viewers.

## 3.2 The Pink Panther: A Symbol of Mischief

The Pink Panther, the cartoon figure that serves as the franchise's unofficial mascot, is as symbolic of the series as Inspector Clouseau himself. Though the animated Pink Panther first debuted in the 1963 film's opening credits, it swiftly became one of the most famous animated characters of the 1960s and 1970s, inspiring a series of cartoons, television specials, and merchandise.

### The Birth of the Animated Panther

The original Pink Panther film's opening scene included an animated Pink Panther. Friz Freleng and his colleagues at DePatie-Freleng Enterprises created the animation to reflect the mischievous spirit of the diamond that serves as the film's central focus. The diamond is reported as having a defect like a panther, however the animated creature was not intended to be a faithful portrayal of the gem. Instead, the animated Pink Panther was a slick, sleek, and amusing creature that exemplified the film's playful and mischievous spirit.

The animated Pink Panther's basic lines and sleek, minimalist look made it immediately identifiable. His elegant motions, smart tactics, and calm attitude made him an ideal counterpart for Clouseau, who was more chaotic and vocally aggressive. The juxtaposition of Clouseau's fumbling ineptitude and the Panther's elegant, almost royal appearance established a dynamic that would become crucial to the franchise's character.

## Mischief & Elegance

Unlike the anarchic Clouseau, the animated Pink Panther had an elegance and refinement that was both amusing and mesmerizing. He was often presented as a prankster—an bright, cunning guy who could outsmart practically any circumstance with ease. Whether he was eluding arrest or merely playing with his pursuers, the Panther was the epitome of calm, calculating mischief.

The Pink Panther's mischievous side was also mirrored in his quiet character. He spoke with motions rather than words, using physical humor and visual puns to convey his message. His absence of conversation made him universal and ageless. His ability to be both charming and deceitful endeared him to people of all ages.

In many respects, the animated Pink Panther represented the polar opposite of the Pink Panther movie' tone. While the movie often focused on Clouseau's fumbling antics, the cartoon Panther was sleek, smart, and seemed in charge. This difference between the two characters became one of the franchise's distinguishing features, demonstrating how comedy could be drawn from both extremes of human (and animated) behavior.

**The Panther as a Popular Culture Icon**

The popularity of the animated Pink Panther prompted the development of a second series of animated shorts that aired throughout the 1960s and 70s. These cartoons depicted the Panther participating in a variety of mischievous escapades, which often included intricate pranks or efforts to outsmart other characters. The animation was simple yet highly stylized, with a flowing, almost jazzy visual style that complimented Henry Mancini's soundtrack. These animations were a break from the typical animated figures of the period, and their simplicity and grace set them apart. The Pink Panther quickly became a cultural sensation, appearing not just in films and television series, but also on goods, ads, and comic strips. His image was associated with coolness and mischief, and he came to represent intellect, elegance, and latent defiance. From his sleek look to his ability to get into and out of trouble, the Pink Panther became a popular character who transcended the realm of film.

## 3.3 Supporting Characters: The Cast of Fools

While Inspector Clouseau and the Pink Panther are the franchise's most recognizable characters, the Pink Panther series would be incomplete without its colorful and often inept supporting ensemble. The films contain a diverse cast of characters, many of whom contribute as much to the story's comedy and turmoil as the main protagonists.

**Dreyfus, the long-suffering boss.**

Clouseau's most memorable exchanges are with his long-suffering employer, Chief Inspector Dreyfus, portrayed by Herbert Lom. Dreyfus is a clever and skilled officer, but his tolerance is often challenged by Clouseau's pranks. While Dreyfus first attempts to manage Clouseau, he quickly becomes obsessed with removing him, which often results in delightfully ridiculous scenarios in which Dreyfus' sanity unravels.

Dreyfus is a fantastic foil for Clouseau. Clouseau's stupidity leads to triumph, but Dreyfus' brilliance and competence seem to lead to calamity. His rising annoyance with Clouseau's antics provides much of the series' comedy, and his out-of-control emotional outbursts make him a noteworthy member of the supporting ensemble.

## Cato Fong, Clouseau's Humble Servant

Burt Kwouk plays Cato Fong, another significant supporting figure. Cato is Clouseau's devoted servant who is often entrusted with keeping Clouseau on his toes by conducting surprise assaults on him to help him remain attentive. Clouseau's contacts with Cato are characterized by awkwardly timed ambushes, which often result in comical violence.

Cato is not only a source of physical humor, but he also plays a key role in demonstrating Clouseau's complete lack of awareness of his surroundings. While Clouseau believes he is always in charge, it is evident that Cato is often the one pulling the strings, arranging his own brand of mayhem. The friendship between Clouseau and Cato is one of the series' more charming parts, with Cato acting as both a counterpoint and a mirror for Clouseau's pranks.

**Marie, the love interest.**

While the Pink Panther flicks are mostly oriented on humor, there is also a touch of romance—primarily in the shape of Marie and Cl

# CHAPTER 4: THE PINK PANTHER'S INFLUENCE ON POP CULTURE

## 4.1 The Panther's Role in Animation and Television

The Pink Panther brand started as a feature film series but swiftly grew into animation, television, and comics. The animated Pink Panther, initially featured in the 1963 film's opening scene, has since become a worldwide pop culture phenomenon, having a long-lasting and deep impact on animation, television, and contemporary entertainment.

**The Animated Pink Panther: A Silent Star.**

The animated Pink Panther made its debut during the opening credits of the original Pink Panther picture. The animated version of the character was sleek, elegant, and mischievous—a far cry from the fumbling, clumsy Inspector Clouseau, but well suited to his function in the series. Without speaking, the cartoon Panther was a mute figure that relied on physical humor, visual jokes, and a captivating personality to swiftly win over viewers. Friz Freleng, the famed animator behind many great cartoons like Looney Tunes, was enlisted to develop and direct the character. The end product was a basic but dynamic design for the Pink Panther, with smooth and fluid motions and antics that were both cute and naughty. The mascot was initially intended to feature as a visual motif in the film, but its rapid success spawned its own animated series, The Pink Panther Show, which debuted in 1969.

The Pink Panther Show is a television sensation.

The popularity of the Pink Panther mascot in the opening credits of the movie spawned a larger television series centered only on the animated panther. The Pink Panther Show, which aired from 1969 to 1978, included a variety of segments, some of which focused on the Pink Panther's antics, while others featured the Inspector (a spoof of Inspector Clouseau) and other colorful characters.

The series helped to establish Pink Panther as a famous cartoon character of the 1970s. In reality, it became one of the most popular Saturday morning cartoons of its period, attracting young viewers with its visual comedy and simple, graceful animation style. While the cartoon format allowed for more abstract and surreal narrative, it nonetheless captured the core of the Pink Panther movie' comedy, with the panther indulging in pranks, capers, and creative problem-solving—all without speaking a word.

One of the character's main appeals was his silence. The absence of words allowed for universal comedy that could transcend language borders, creating Pink Panther a globally famous figure. His elegance, mixed with his mischievous nature, made him immediately recognized, and his television escapades established his status as one of animation's most popular characters.

## Expanding the Animated Universe.

As the Pink Panther Show became famous, it spawned several animated shows and specials. In the years since the initial program, there have been several spinoffs and adaptations, including new Pink Panther cartoons and adaptations for other mediums, such as TV specials and animated features. The character was so popular that even during times of diminished exposure in cinema, the Pink Panther remained active on television and in the realm of animation.

The character's popularity resurged in the 1990s, resulting in the release of new animated programs such as The Pink Panther and Pals (2010). These series attempted to introduce the character to a new generation, although with modernized graphics and narrative techniques. Nonetheless, the heart of the Pink Panther's allure—his slick, quiet comedy and ageless appeal—remained vital to his portrayal.

The Impact of Animation

The cartoon Pink Panther had a huge impact on the whole landscape of animated television. His minimalist approach and emphasis on physical comedy laid the groundwork for subsequent animated characters, especially those that expressed individuality via motion rather than words. While Looney Tunes and Tom and Jerry had previously pioneered slapstick humor in animation, Pink Panther introduced a more sophisticated, laid-back style that appealed to both children and adults.

Furthermore, the animation of the Pink Panther was innovative for its day. The character's beautiful, flowing motions exemplified the beauty of traditional animation, but his humorous timing and visual jokes established new standards for cartoon comedy. The Pink Panther's effect may be seen in following animated series such as The Pink Panther and Pals, Dexter's Laboratory, and The Simpsons, where physical comedy and exaggerated gestures have helped to create unique animated characters.

## 4.2 Pink Panther's Legacy in Advertising

The Pink Panther character's effect goes well beyond television and movies. Since his debut in 1963, the Pink Panther has featured in a variety of advertising campaigns, using his naughty charm and exquisite character to sell items in an entertaining and memorable manner. The character's connection with elegance, flair, and comedy made him an excellent figure for marketers to use in a variety of sectors, including food, apparel, and technology.

**The first Pink Panther commercials**

The Pink Panther's first notable entrance into advertising was in the 1970s, when the character became a crucial role in the promotion of many items. His visual attractiveness, sleekness, and impish charm make him an excellent pick for businesses seeking to reach a large audience. One of the first uses of the Pink Panther in advertising was by Eagle Snacks, which featured the character in a series of adverts to appeal to a younger clientele.

The Pink Panther has also appeared in promotional materials for big organizations, such as British Petroleum (BP), where the mascot was utilized to promote the company's services. The commercial campaign relied on the panther's connotation with elegance and refinement, linking these attributes to the BP brand. This was the beginning of the Pink Panther's long-lasting presence in advertising.

The Pink Panther: Product Endorsement

Over time, the Pink Panther became a familiar face in advertising, promoting everything from M&Ms to clothing lines and even cars. His ability to cross linguistic and cultural boundaries made him an ideal mascot for a worldwide marketplace, and his quiet demeanor enabled companies to reach a wide spectrum of customers.

In a hugely successful advertising campaign in the 1990s, the Pink Panther became the face of Peugeot vehicles. The advertisements, which showcased the Pink Panther's antics as he interacted with the automobiles, boosted the vehicle's image while also cementing the Panther's status as a worldwide pop culture phenomenon.

In the 1980s and 1990s, the Pink Panther's image appeared in advertisements for a broad range of consumer products, including Wrigley's chewing gum and Mercedes-Benz. His image was adaptable enough to suit a wide range of product categories, from the inexpensive and whimsical to the opulent and refined. As a consequence, the Pink Panther became associated with both elegance and humour, making him an effective marketing tool for firms looking to project an aspirational but playful image.

The Pink Panther: A Symbol of Sophistication

The Pink Panther's continued appearance in advertisements indicates his link with flair, elegance, and cheekiness. His smart but amusing personality has enabled him to be employed in a variety of sectors, including fashion, cuisine, and technology. For example, in 2009, the mascot featured in a Swarovski campaign, where the premium crystal company used the panther's image to reinforce the high-end, trendy image of its goods. Similarly, the mascot has featured in branding for big stores and even video game companies, always exuding an aura of sophistication and naughty charm.

## Enduring Popular Culture Influence

The Pink Panther's position in advertising exemplifies a larger tendency in pop culture, in which famous characters transcend their original context and become icons for a variety of commercial items. The panther's capacity to easily adapt to new marketing efforts has guaranteed that his influence extends well beyond the bounds of the Pink Panther movie. His continuing use in advertising demonstrates the enduring power of famous, fashionable figures in pop culture, as well as how they can be utilized to convey stories and establish corporate identification.

4.3 Parodies and Homages in Modern Media.

Over the years, the Pink Panther series has inspired various parodies, homages, and allusions in current culture. From animated shows to films and even stand-up comedy, the character has impacted innumerable creative who have drawn inspiration from the Pink Panther's particular style, humor, and personality.

**Parodies in movies and television**

The Pink Panther series has been imitated in a number of films and television programs, with comedians and writers paying tribute to the character's distinct combination of humor and elegance. One famous example is Austin Powers: International Man of Mystery (1997), which closely references the Pink Panther flicks in its portrayal of a clumsy, inept investigator (played by Mike Myers) who is constantly one step behind the action. Austin Powers and Inspector Clouseau have comparable wacky personalities, outlandish equipment, and over-the-top performances.

Other parodies of the Pink Panther may be seen in famous TV series such as The Simpsons and Family Guy, where the characters often mock Clouseau's ineptness or make visual allusions to the Pink Panther. The Pink Panther theme has also appeared in several TV and film parodies, solidifying the character's standing as a cultural icon.

## Homages in Music and Arts

Henry Mancini's renowned Pink Panther theme is often utilized as a reference point in current music and art, demonstrating the franchise's long-lasting impact. The theme has been sampled and recorded by performers from numerous genres, including jazz and pop, and its distinctive melody remains a recognized icon of the Pink Panther in popular culture.

Artists have also paid tribute to the figure in visual art, creating pieces that evoke the panther's sleek shape and minimalist look. The character's timeless appeal has inspired a broad variety of creative adaptations, from current pop art to graphic design, with the panther maintaining a symbol of refinement, mischief, and humor.

## The Enduring Legacy

The Pink Panther's influence in contemporary media reflects the character's distinct combination of refinement, wit, and naughty charm. His effect on animation, advertising, and pop culture is still felt today, and he is regarded as one of the most iconic individuals in entertainment history. Pink Panther continues to inspire and excite new generations of fans while being a cherished cultural icon, thanks to parodies, homages, and allusions in current media.

# CHAPTER 5: THE VISUAL APPEAL: ART AND DESIGN

## 5.1 The Pink Panther's Distinctive Animation Style

The Pink Panther franchise is as much a visual journey as it is a comedic one. From the opening titles of the first film in 1963 to the animated series that followed, the Pink Panther's design has stood out as one of the most iconic and easily recognizable styles in animation history. In this section, we'll explore the elements that define the Panther's visual aesthetic and what makes his design both timeless and impactful.

### 5.1.1 The Minimalist Aesthetic

The Pink Panther's animation style is an embodiment of minimalist design. Unlike many animated characters, who are often exaggerated in their features, the Pink Panther's sleek, elongated body and smooth, clean lines set him apart. His design emphasizes elegance and simplicity—key elements that have helped him transcend generations and become a lasting cultural icon.

This minimalist approach was introduced by Friz Freleng, who took inspiration from the elegance of classic animation, using simple forms and movements to convey a sense of sophistication. Unlike the often frenetic action of cartoons like Looney Tunes or Tom and Jerry, the Pink Panther's visual style was cool, controlled, and fluid. This decision to emphasize visual economy—reducing unnecessary detail and focusing on core expressive traits—helped to solidify the Panther's smooth, almost regal persona.

## 5.1.2 Fluidity in Movement

One of the most distinct aspects of the Pink Panther's animation style is the fluidity of his movements. The character's walk, his interactions with his environment, and his facial expressions (which often don't need to be exaggerated to communicate emotion) all follow a smooth, flowing rhythm. The Panther's movements were designed to evoke a sense of grace and control, perfectly in line with his status as an effortlessly cool and mischievous character.

The animation's pacing is equally important—timing and subtlety create the humor that is the hallmark of the Panther's character. His deliberate movements, whether it be a slow-motion glance or a sophisticated paw swipe, become comedic through their contrast to the hectic, slapstick nature of the world around him. In essence, the Panther's design and movements suggest a high level of intelligence, sophistication, and wit—qualities that make his mischief even more amusing.

### 5.1.3 The Use of Color

The choice of the color pink for the character is another essential element of the Panther's visual identity. Pink, often associated with softness, femininity, and gentleness, is paradoxically the color of a character who is sly, clever, and mischievous. This contradiction between his soft, approachable color and his sharp, cunning personality plays a significant role in defining his character.

The Pink Panther's design is complemented by a harmonious use of color throughout his world. The backgrounds, the other characters, and even the situations he finds himself in are all carefully crafted to maintain a certain visual balance. The visual simplicity of the Pink Panther universe allows the character to shine brightly in contrast, becoming the focal point of every scene.

## 5.2 Set Design and Cinematic Aesthetics

While the animated Pink Panther stands as a paragon of design in the world of cartoons, the live-action Pink Panther films also present a world rich in visual storytelling and cinematic aesthetics. The set design and the overall look of the films were integral in building the franchise's distinct atmosphere—an atmosphere that combined elegance with absurdity.

### 5.2.1 The Sleek and Stylish World of Clouseau

The Pink Panther films, particularly those starring Peter Sellers as Inspector Clouseau, are defined by a unique blend of sophistication and comedic absurdity. The lavish settings and luxurious environments help establish a tone of high society, wealth, and class. These opulent settings—whether in a grand hotel, a lavish estate, or a high-profile party—form the backdrop for Clouseau's clumsy, often disastrous antics.

The film's set designers used these settings not only to create an air of affluence but also to highlight the character of Clouseau and the contrast between his bumbling nature and the refined world he inhabits. The mise-en-scène is often meticulously planned to enhance this juxtaposition. For example, Clouseau's frequent inability to blend into these luxurious environments is visually underscored by the contrast between his chaotic presence and the sleek, composed surroundings.

## 5.2.2 The Visual Language of the Films

The aesthetic choices in the Pink Panther films go beyond set design and extend to the overall visual language. Cinematographer Geoffrey Unsworth, who worked on the first few films, played a key role in developing a look that combined a sense of lavishness with the understated elegance of classic Hollywood.

Many scenes in the Pink Panther films use the power of visual gags to tell a story. The framing of the scenes often emphasizes the absurdity of Clouseau's presence within these high-society environments. Close-up shots of the character's face, where his confusion and incompetence are exaggerated, serve to highlight the contrast between his character and the world around him. The lavish décor and costumes also contribute to the films' visual style—luxury is depicted as cold and elegant, yet in stark contrast with Clouseau's comically unrefined nature.

The lighting in the Pink Panther films also plays a significant role in creating a sense of opulence. Soft lighting is often used to bathe the settings in a glamorous glow, while more direct, hard lighting is used to emphasize moments of comedic tension. This play between light and shadow often mirrors the characters' own dualities—Clouseau's lack of awareness versus his belief in his own brilliance, for example.

### 5.2.3 The Role of Color in Set Design

Color, too, plays a pivotal role in the set design and cinematic aesthetics of the Pink Panther films. Much like the character himself, the films make use of bright, bold colors to create a sense of playfulness and wit. The costumes, furniture, and overall set decoration frequently employ vivid colors to reinforce the comedic and whimsical tone of the franchise.

For instance, the interiors of the various estates and high-class settings in the films are often filled with rich tones—gold, silver, deep blues, and vibrant reds—that visually suggest wealth and sophistication. These colors help set the scene for the comedy that unfolds, heightening the absurdity of the situations the characters find themselves in.

The Pink Panther itself, with its unique, contrasting hue, often acts as an accent within these settings, standing out vividly against the more muted tones of the surroundings. This clever use of color emphasizes the presence of the Panther as a symbol of both elegance and mischief, occupying a world that's both refined and just a little bit absurd.

---

## 5.3 The Evolution of the Panther's Visual Identity

The Pink Panther's visual identity has evolved considerably since his first appearance in 1963, adapting to changing tastes, technological advances, and the character's growing presence across different mediums. From the early days of the character's creation to the more modern depictions in animated series, films, and other media, the visual identity of the Pink Panther has undergone a number of notable changes.

### 5.3.1 The Original Design

The original design of the Pink Panther, as created by Friz Freleng and his team at DePatie-Freleng

Enterprises, was intentionally simple, relying on smooth lines and minimalistic features to convey the character's personality. The lack of extraneous detail and the clean, sleek design made him instantly recognizable.

The early Pink Panther design was meant to evoke a sense of elegance and grace, with subtle humor embedded in the character's movements and actions. His color, a soft yet striking pink, was also a defining characteristic, chosen to make him stand out in a world filled with more traditionally designed animated characters. The original design set the tone for the Panther's future appearance in various forms of media, creating an icon that could exist both as a smooth, intelligent character and a playful, mischievous figure.

## 5.3.2 Changes in the Animated Series

As the Pink Panther transitioned from film to television in the 1960s, his visual design remained largely the same, but the demands of television animation required some adjustments. In particular, the character's movements were refined to allow for quicker production and smoother animation. The early Pink Panther Show cartoons retained much of the minimalist design, but the animation itself became more exaggerated, giving the character more freedom to express himself through action and physical comedy.

The show's creative team expanded the Panther's visual identity by incorporating more detailed backgrounds and adding new characters into the mix. The visual style of the animated series was influenced by the rise of modern animation techniques, but the core elements of the Panther's design remained true to his original form. Even as technology advanced, the simplicity of the character's visual design allowed him to remain timeless and instantly recognizable.

### 5.3.3 The Evolution of the Panther's Design in

### Modern Media

In the 1990s and 2000s, as the Pink Panther franchise saw a resurgence through new animated series, films, and merchandise, the character's design began to evolve once again. These new depictions of the Pink Panther incorporated more modern animation styles, often with bolder lines and slightly more exaggerated features. However, the character's essence remained unchanged—he was still the same sleek, smooth, and mischievous panther who had won audiences' hearts decades earlier.

# CHAPTER 6: THE PINK PANTHER SOUNDTRACK AND MUSIC

## 6.1. The Pink Panther's distinct animation style

The Pink Panther film series is a visual and comedic journey. The Pink Panther's design has become one of the most recognized and instantly recognizable designs in animation history, beginning with the opening credits of the first film in 1963 and continuing through the animated series that followed. In this section, we'll look at the Panther's visual appeal and what makes his design so classic and stunning.

### 5.1.1 The Minimalist Aesthetic

The Pink Panther's animation style is a classic example of minimalist design. Unlike many cartoon animals with exaggerated traits, the Pink Panther sticks out with his sleek, stretched body and smooth, clean contours. His design focuses on beauty and simplicity, which has enabled him to transcend decades and become a cultural icon.

Friz Freleng invented the minimalist approach, borrowing inspiration from the elegance of classical animation and used simple forms and actions to create a sense of refinement. Unlike the usually chaotic action of cartoons like Looney Tunes or Tom and Jerry, the Pink Panther's visual style was quiet, controlled, and smooth. This decision to favor visual economy—reducing unnecessary detail and focusing on core expressive traits—aided the Panther's flowing, almost regal appearance.

## 5.1.2 Fluidity in Motion.

Pink Panther's animation style is distinguished by the fluidity with which he moves. The character's movement, interactions with his environment, and facial expressions (which seldom need exaggeration to indicate emotion) all follow a smooth, flowing rhythm. The Panther's movements were designed to portray a sense of grace and strength, which complemented his image as an effortlessly cool and mischievous character.

The animation's speed is also significant—timing and subtlety create the humor that distinguishes the Panther's persona. In contrast to the chaotic, comic nature of the world around him, his meticulous motions, like as a slow-motion look or a deft paw swipe, seem amusing. In essence, the Panther's design and movements suggest a high level of intelligence, sophistication, and wit—qualities that make his disobedience all the more amusing.

## 5.1.3 Use of Color

The Panther's usage of the color pink is also a significant part of his visual identity. Pink, which is often associated with softness, delicacy, and compassion, is really the color of a character who is crafty, sly, and mischievous. The contrast between his soft, welcoming hue and his sharp, intelligent manner serves to establish his personality.

The Pink Panther's design is enhanced by the continuous use of color throughout his surroundings. The surroundings, other people, and even the situation he finds himself in are all deliberately planned to maintain a precise visual balance. The visual simplicity of the Pink Panther universe allows the character to stand out in every scene.

## 5.2 Set Design and Cinematic

## Aesthetic.

While the animated Pink Panther is a design landmark in the world of cartoons, the live-action Pink Panther films provide a visually rich story and cinematic aesthetics. The film's set design and overall style were crucial in defining the franchise's distinct mood, which combined elegance with absurdity.

## 5.2.1 Clouseau's Sleek and Stylish World

The Pink Panther films, particularly those starring Peter Sellers as Inspector Clouseau, are defined by a unique blend of sophistication and comedic lunacy. The lavish settings and luxurious places add to the feeling of high society, wealth, and position. These lavish settings—whether at a grand hotel, a rich estate, or a high-profile party—set the stage for Clouseau's clumsy, occasionally catastrophic pranks.

The film's set designers used these settings not just to portray an air of wealth, but also to highlight Clouseau's character and the contrast between his clumsy nature and the polished surroundings in which he lives. The mise-en-scene is often designed to underline this discrepancy. The contrast between Clouseau's wild presence and the spotless, regulated surroundings emphasizes his repeated inability to fit into these privileged environments.

## 5.2.2 The Visual Language of Film.

The artistic considerations in the Pink Panther film extend beyond set design to cover the whole visual language. Cinematographer Geoffrey Unsworth, who worked on the first few films, was essential in developing a style that combined a sense of opulence with the delicate grace of classic Hollywood.

Many scenes in the Pink Panther movies depend on visual gags to tell a story. The movie' framing often highlights Clouseau's absurd appearance in these high-society surroundings. Close-ups of the character's face highlight his confusion and inadequacy, accentuating the difference between himself and the world around him. The lavish décor and clothing also contribute to the film's visual style—luxury is shown as frigid and elegant, in stark contrast to Clouseau's wonderfully unpolished personality.

The lighting in the Pink Panther film adds much to the sense of richness. Soft lighting is often utilized to give sets a sumptuous gloss, whilst harsh, rough lighting is used to heighten comedic tension. This dance between light and shadow often represents the characters' inner dichotomies—Clouseau's lack of awareness contrasted with his faith in his own brilliance, for example.

## 5.2.3 The Application of Color in Set Design

Color is also used extensively in the Pink Panther film's set design and cinematic style. Much like the character, the films use bright, colorful colors to portray a sense of joy and amusement. Bright colors are often used in the franchise's clothing, furniture, and overall set décor to underline its comedic and whimsical tone.

For example, the interiors of the film's many estates and high-class settings are often painted in rich tones—gold, silver, deep blues, and dazzling reds—that visually suggest wealth and elegance. These colors help to set the tone for the subsequent comedy, underlining the absurdity of the protagonists' situation.

The Pink Panther's unusual, contrasting hue often acts as an accent in these settings, standing out starkly against the more moderate tones of the surroundings. This magnificent use of color emphasizes the Panther's position as a symbol of both elegance and mischief, occupying a gorgeous but little comical world.

## 5.3 Creation of Panther's Visual

## Identity

Since his first appearance in 1963, the Pink Panther's visual identity has evolved dramatically to suit changing tastes, technological improvements, and the character's growing popularity across several media. The Pink Panther's visual identity has evolved substantially over time, from its conception to more recent appearances in animated series, films, and other media.

## 5.3.1 Original Design.

Friz Freleng and his team at DePatie-Freleng Enterprises created the Pink Panther's first design with the intention of keeping it simple, concentrating on flowing lines and minimalist qualities to convey the spirit of the character. The lack of extraneous detail, along with his clean, streamlined appearance, made him immediately identifiable.

The early Pink Panther design aimed to express a sense of elegance and grace, with subtle humor hidden in the character's movements and actions. His color, a delicate yet striking pink, was also a distinctive trait, chosen to set him out in a world full of more traditionally rendered animated characters. The Panther's original design set the tone for his subsequent appearance in a variety of media, creating a mark that could be both a sleek, smart character and a fun, mischievous figure.

## 5.3.2 Changes in the Animated Series

As the Pink Panther transitioned from film to television in the 1960s, his visual look remained mostly similar, although the limits of television animation required certain alterations. The character's movements were deliberately altered to allow for speedier manufacturing and improved animation. The early Pink Panther Show cartoons retained much of its fundamental design, but the animation became more exaggerated, enabling the character to express himself more freely via movement and physical comedy.

The show's design team improved the Panther's visual identity by including more intricate settings and new characters. The visual style of the animated series was influenced by advancements in modern animation techniques, although the core aspects of the Panther's design remained intact with his original look. Despite technology developments, the character's visual appearance remained timeless and easy to recognize.

### 5.3.3 The Evolution of the Panther's Image in Modern Media

When the Pink Panther brand returned in the 1990s and 2000s with new animated series, films, and goods, the character's appearance began to evolve once again. These new Pink Panther interpretations employed more modern animation techniques, such as bolder lines and somewhat exaggerated features. However, the character's foundation remained unchanged—he was still the same sleek, suave, and mischievous panther who had won viewers' hearts decades ago.

In later iterations, particularly in digital media, the figure has gained more sophisticated textures and three-dimensional properties. The most recent designs also reflect advances in animation technology, with the Panther's movements becoming smoother and his surroundings more detailed. Despite these technological advancements, the fundamental ideals of his design—simplicity, elegance, and mischief—have remained the basic pillars.

# CHAPTER 7: PINK PANTHER BEYOND FILM

While the Pink Panther series originated on the big screen, its cultural impact stretches well beyond that. The Pink Panther has evolved into a multifaceted emblem of entertainment and popular culture, with television spin-offs and computer games, as well as a vast selection of goods. This chapter delves into the Pink Panther's effect outside of film, concentrating on its extension into television, video games, and merchandise, as well as its ongoing cultural importance.

## 7.1 Spin-off TV shows and specials

The success of the Pink Panther flicks, notably the famous opening credits sequence and the figure of the Pink Panther, opened the door for a number of spin-offs. These television episodes and specials took the character's spirit and stretched it into other media, enabling the franchise to reach new audiences and remain relevant for decades after its film premiere.

## 7.1.1 The Pink Panther Show (1969-1978)

The first big television spin-off, The Pink Panther Show, debuted in 1969. This cartoon series introduced the figure of the Pink Panther to the foreground, having previously only appeared briefly in the opening credits of films. The program concentrated around the mischievous escapades of the Pink Panther, who often found himself in situations involving slapstick comedy and exaggerated antics, much like his film counterpart. Unlike the films, which centered on Inspector Clouseau's humor and crime-solving, the television series had a more episodic, cartoon-style approach. The Pink Panther was characterized as a quiet, cold guy, and many episodes had him attempting to outsmart different opponents or escape hilarious situations. The show's premise enabled the Pink

Panther to grow beyond his initial position, and his personality was shown via his actions rather than speaking. This made the show more accessible to audiences of all ages, especially youngsters, while yet keeping the character's charm and wit.

## 7.1.2 Pink Panther and Sons (1984–1985)

Pink Panther and Sons, a fresh spin on the character, premiered on television in 1984. This series portrayed the Pink Panther as a father figure to his young offspring. The program, which was mainly aimed at children, had a more family-friendly plot, with the Pink Panther's children participating in numerous adventures that were often more touching than the traditional slapstick humor.

The animated series deviated from the usual silent character of the Pink Panther by giving his youngsters more significant personalities and language. However, the series maintained the whimsical tone of the original cartoons, integrating the Panther into a more realistic family dynamic while retaining the joyful, adventurous attitude that viewers adored. Despite not being as successful as the other programs, Pink Panther and Sons brought the character to a new generation of fans.

## 7.1.3 Pink Panther Specials

In addition to the television series, various animated television specials were created to extend the universe of the Pink Panther. These specials, which were often telecast around holidays or on special occasions, showed the Panther going on new adventures. These specials were often a continuation of the original movie' comedy and flair, emphasizing the Panther's ability to outsmart people and wreak mischief while keeping his calm demeanor.

The most renowned of these specials is A Pink Christmas (1978), which evoked the holiday mood with a playful, joyous tale. Another notable special was The Pink Panther in Pink at First Sight (1995), which was part of a campaign to reintroduce the character to a more contemporary audience. These specials cemented the character's presence in the larger television scene, assuring that the Pink Panther's popularity would not be limited to the cinema.

## 7.2 Panther's Role in Video Games

The Pink Panther series thrived not just on television and film, but also in video games. Over the years, the Pink Panther has appeared in a number of video game adaptations, where his cool, cheeky nature makes him a popular figure for interactive entertainment.

### 7.2.1 The Pink Panther Video Game's Beginnings

The first video game featuring the Pink Panther was launched in 1982 on the Atari 2600. The Pink Panther game was a basic arcade-style game in which players guided the Panther over numerous obstacles. Though basic by today's standards, this early video game brought the character to a new media, enabling fans to connect with the Panther in ways they hadn't before.

The popularity of the early Pink Panther games prompted future versions for a variety of platforms, including the Commodore 64 and Amiga. These games were mostly adventure-based, with the Pink Panther having to solve puzzles or perform chores to progress. The games often focused on the Panther's quiet, stealthy character, stressing stealth and intelligence in overcoming hurdles. Though these early games were not innovative in terms of gameplay, they were an efficient way to expand the Pink Panther brand beyond cinema and television.

## 7.2.2 The Pink Panther's Passport to Peril (1996)

The Pink Panther: Passport to Peril for PC, one of the most popular and well-known video game adaptations of the character, was released in 1996. In this game, the player takes on the role of the Pink Panther, who goes on a global expedition to stop a jewel thief. The game combined standard point-and-click adventure features with puzzle solving, and also included a variety of mini-games that fit the franchise's cheerful tone.

Passport to Peril received accolades for its intriguing gameplay and accurate portrayal of the Pink Panther persona. It caught the essence of the movie, focusing on smart humor and nonverbal comedy to immerse players in the Panther universe. The game's distinct combination of adventure, exploration, and humor introduced the Pink Panther to the realm of interactive entertainment, appealing to both film enthusiasts and newbies to the character.

## 7.2.3 More Current Pink Panther Games

While the Pink Panther brand had a smaller video game presence than other prominent media properties, the games released in the 1990s and early 2000s functioned as important points of contact between the character and consumers. More recent efforts to return the Panther to gaming have been less successful, however titles such as The

Pink Panther: The Party (2005) and Pink Panther: Pinkadelic Pursuit (2004) sought to emulate the original flicks' charm and wit.

## 7.3 Merchandise and Cultural Impact.

The Pink Panther franchise has long been connected with a wide range of goods, which has kept the character in the public eye. The Pink Panther has been marketed in a variety of ways, including toys, apparel, home goods, and collectibles, making him one of the most famous figures in popular culture.

### 7.3.1 Pink Panther Toys and Collectibles.

Pink Panther has appeared in several toy lines since his introduction. These toys included plush animals, action figures, board games, and puzzles. Early toys emphasized the character's sleek, naughty characteristics, with many having his signature pink hue and comfortable, cool manner. As the brand grew, so did the merchandise, with a diverse range of toys and memorabilia being available from different merchants.

The Pink Panther was often advertised as a figure for both children and adults. Adult collectors were particularly drawn to the limited edition items, which featured sculptures, plush dolls, and historical memorabilia. These souvenirs are still in great demand today, thanks to the character's enduring appeal in pop culture, which ensures a continual supply of items.

## 7.3.2 The Panther's Iconic Image in Merchandise

The Pink Panther's trademark image—a sleek, anthropomorphic cat with a cool demeanor—has appeared on a wide range of commercial items, including clothes and accessories, as well as home goods and appliances. His unusual style, paired with his fun, suave nature, has made him a popular image on everything from t-shirts and mugs to bed linens and kitchenware.

The Pink Panther's relationship with coolness and flair made him an obvious choice for branded products. He has featured on a wide range of things, including fragrances, watches, and even autos. His image has been changed and remade innumerable times to keep up with shifting trends, yet his core attraction has stayed steady throughout generations.

## 7.3.3 Cultural Impact and Persistent Popularity

The cultural significance of the Pink Panther cannot be emphasized. From his impact on fashion and design to his standing as a symbol of coolness and mischief, the Pink Panther has been ingrained in popular culture. His unusual look and cheeky nature have established him as a symbol of wit, refinement, and lighthearted comedy.

The Pink Panther's ongoing presence in the media—via products, ads, and pop culture references—ensures that his legacy endures. He has become a timeless emblem of both elegance and irreverence, and his popularity shows no signs of slowing. The cultural significance of Pink Panther is apparent, whether via the continuous popularity of his animated series, his presence in pop culture, or his continued merchandise success..

# CHAPTER 8: REBOOT & REVIVAL.

The Pink Panther series has had multiple revivals throughout the years, with various variations of the character appearing in new forms and situations. From the 2000s remake of the flicks to the franchise's continued promise, the Pink Panther has proven to be a figure with long-term appeal. This chapter looks at the Pink Panther franchise's rebirth in the 2000s, the influence of this new generation of films on both older and younger viewers, and the character's future in cinema, television, and popular culture.

## 8.1 The 2000s Reboot and its

## Reception

The Pink Panther series, which had been inactive for over two decades, was revitalized in the 2000s with the production of a new film, The Pink Panther (2006). This relaunch was a substantial shift from the original series in terms of tone and style, concentrating on modernizing the character for a new generation of fans while remaining true to the franchise's hilarious past.

## 8.1.1 Reboot's Approach

The idea to relaunch the Pink Panther series in the 2000s was prompted by Hollywood's rising appetite for nostalgia-based reboots. Given the popularity of remakes of iconic films from previous decades, it seemed like a logical step to bring back a renowned comedy character from the 1960s and 1970s. However, rather of merely continuing Inspector Clouseau's plot or reviving the same characters and comedy, the directors sought to recreate the series for contemporary viewers.

Shawn Levy directed the 2006 picture The Pink Panther, which stars Steve Martin as the bumbling Inspector Jacques Clouseau. Martin's interpretation of Clouseau differed from Peter Sellers' original, opting for a more exaggerated, farcical version of the character while retaining some of the renowned predecessor's basic qualities. The narrative focuses on an inquiry into the death of a well-known soccer coach and the theft of the Pink Panther diamond. While Steve Martin's depiction of Clouseau divided fans, the film tried to uphold the franchise's tradition of humor and intrigue. The revamped picture had a more contemporary, action-oriented narrative while attempting to maintain the original movie' charm, notably via the use of physical humor and visual jokes.

## 8.1.2 Critical Reception

The 2006 Pink Panther revival garnered mixed reviews from reviewers. On the one hand, many people enjoyed the film's joyful tone, slapstick humor, and Steve Martin's physical comedy, which reminded them of the original Clouseau. Many critics, however, believed that the picture failed to capture the character's distinct charm and humor, which Peter Sellers had brought to life. Sellers' interpretation was famous for its delicacy and elegance, while Martin's Clouseau was larger and more exaggerated in character.

Critics commented that the picture lacked some of the cerebral comedy and sophisticated jokes that distinguished the 1960s Pink Panther features. However, the picture was a financial triumph, grossing more than $160 million worldwide, demonstrating that the Pink Panther is still in demand in today's cinematic environment. Despite conflicting reviews, the film's popularity justified a sequel.

## 8.1.3 Pink Panther 2 (2009).

Following the popularity of the original remake, The Pink Panther 2 was released in 2009, and Steve Martin reprised his role as Clouseau. The sequel maintained the same comic tone as its predecessor, with the clumsy Inspector Clouseau tasked with solving the theft of a rare relic. While The Pink Panther 2 was a box office triumph, generating over

$75 million, it received even more unfavorable reviews than the original picture. Critics were especially critical of the film's repetitious and formulaic style, claiming it lacked the uniqueness of the 2006 feature.

Despite these scathing reviews, the Pink Panther remake and sequel brought the character to a new generation of admirers, particularly younger viewers who were unfamiliar with the original movie. The films leaned on Steve Martin's star power and ability to create wide comic performances, ensuring that the series remained relevant in contemporary Hollywood.

## 8.2 The Next Generation of Pink Panther Fans

The 2000s reboots brought the Pink Panther to a new generation, with younger audiences encountering the legendary character for the first time via the films. While the films were not uniformly well received by reviewers, they introduced the character to a larger audience and helped the Pink Panther series retain its cultural relevance.

## 8.2.1 The Importance of Modern Media

The 2000s revival of the Pink Panther films benefitted from the advent of digital media and online streaming services, allowing the films to reach a larger audience than they had before. Digital services like as Netflix, Amazon Prime, and Hulu made the movie available to worldwide audiences, ensuring that the character remained accessible to people from all over the globe. This allowed the Pink Panther brand to remain relevant even as younger generations of consumers grew up with alternative types of entertainment.

In addition to streaming, the rise of social media sites like as YouTube and Instagram helped the Pink Panther become a meme-worthy figure, with brief snippets, GIFs, and phrases from the relaunched flicks becoming viral. The hilarity and absurdity of Steve Martin's Clouseau found a new home in the realm of viral material, and the character's famous theme tune was often utilized in comedic situations, cementing the Pink Panther's place in digital culture.

## 8.2.2 Merchandise and License

The relaunch also resulted in a rise in item sales, as younger fans found Pink Panther via the new flicks. The character was reintroduced to the market with new apparel lines, toys, video games, and collectibles, broadening the franchise's consumer product offerings. The Pink Panther's prominence as a revered symbol enabled this kind of cross-generational appeal, allowing both older and younger fans to enjoy the character in various ways. In particular, the Pink Panther film series had a major impact on fashion in the 2000s, when the character's cool, suave image made him a popular icon for items in the lifestyle and clothing area. T-shirts, backpacks, and accessories portraying the Pink Panther were popular among a contemporary audience who regarded him as a symbol of fashionable mischief.

# 8.3 The Future of the Franchise

Despite the negative reviews of the 2000s remake flicks, the Pink Panther brand has the potential for further rebirth and innovation. There are various options for reintroducing the character to current audiences, ensuring that the Pink Panther's legacy lives on for years to come.

## 8.3.1 Upcoming Projects and Potential Reboot

There have been various stories throughout the years indicating that Hollywood is still interested in expanding the Pink Panther brand. A new Pink Panther film was announced in 2020, with Rian Johnson, director of Knives Out, apparently in discussions to helm the next series. This remake is planned to modernize the series while preserving the original flicks' comic history. The participation of Johnson, famed for his snappy language and complicated plotting, fueled hopes that the upcoming Pink Panther picture will take the character to intriguing new areas, maybe with a greater focus on mystery and intrigue.

In addition, there has been persistent talk regarding an animated series or a fresh wave of merchandise. As pop culture evolves and the desire for nostalgic material grows, the Pink Panther could easily find a home on streaming services such as Netflix or Disney+ as a remade series or as part of an anthology of historic cartoons and movies.

## 8.3.2 Continued Appeal in Global Markets.

The Pink Panther series has always had worldwide appeal, and with the expansion of global markets in Asia and Latin America, the character's popularity may rise even more. A new Pink Panther project might appeal to these groups by localizing and culturally adapting the character while retaining the key elements that make it worldwide recognized.

The ongoing emergence of foreign streaming services such as Netflix and Amazon Prime increases the possibility for the Pink Panther series to expand internationally. With digital distribution, the character is no longer limited to a single market or language, allowing multinational audiences to interact with the character in their own unique manner.

## 8.3.3 A New Era for the Pink Panther.

The Pink Panther franchise's future looks bright, as the character's ageless charm and sense of mischief continue to captivate fans of all ages. Whether via a relaunched film, a new animated series, or a reworking of the character for contemporary media, the Pink Panther is certain to be a lasting cultural icon.

# CHAPTER 9: THE ENDURING CHARM OF THE PINK PANTHER.

The Pink Panther has been a revered cultural symbol for more than 50 years. From his naughty antics and suave manner to his ability to transcend time and trends, the Pink Panther is an enduring icon of humor, charm, and fun. This chapter digs into why the Pink Panther continues to attract viewers and how his legacy transcends decades, cultures, and changing entertainment landscapes.

## 9.1 Why the Pink Panther Still Captures Audiences.

The Pink Panther's popularity stems from its distinct combination of humor, elegance, and timelessness. This section delves into the essential characteristics that make the character and series so compelling.

# 9.1.1 Universal Humor and Appeal.

The Pink Panther's universal comedy is one of the reasons it continues to attract audiences today. Whether via mischievous pranks, physical humor, or silent shenanigans, the Pink Panther connects with his audience in a manner that goes beyond words. The character's visual comedy and humorous gestures appeal to audiences all around the globe, making him a cross-cultural figure capable of eliciting laughter regardless of geography or language.

The absence of speaking in the early animated shorts and features contributes significantly to the character's worldwide appeal. Without words, the Pink Panther's behaviors portray a widely accessible narrative. His silent comedy follows in the footsteps of silent cinema giants like as Charlie Chaplin and Buster Keaton, who used physicality to express humor that anybody, regardless of background, could appreciate.

## 9.1.2 The Cool Factor.

The Pink Panther's identity has always been about flair and refinement, which lends him a certain attraction. Even as a cartoon character, he emanates coolness and a casual demeanor that make him immediately recognizable. This laid-back but suave manner has kept the Pink Panther relevant in today's contemporary culture, where coolness is still a desirable characteristic.

The Panther's attractiveness stems not just from his sleek pink shape and graceful motions, but also from his confidence. In many ways, the Pink Panther exemplifies easy style. Whether he's solving riddles or merely avoiding capture, his calm and self-assured demeanor is a big element of his charm.

## 9.1.3 Ageless Comedy

The humor of the Pink Panther is based on physicality, slapstick, and visual gags—comedy that has endured for centuries. This style of humor's simplicity makes the character approachable and pleasant to both young and elderly viewers. While some of the pop culture allusions and societal background from the previous Pink Panther flicks may have become antiquated, the physical humor remains ageless.

The Pink Panther's antics—whether he's sneaking about or escaping his inept antagonist, Inspector Clouseau—are still relevant today. In a world where humor is often influenced by fads, the Pink Panther's form of global, visual comedy has proved to be astonishingly timeless. His attractiveness is not based on language, rendering him impervious to the transient character of current comedy.

## 9.1.4 Nostalgia Factor.

For many individuals, the Pink Panther evokes childhood recollections or good memories of family movie nights. The character's timeless charm and nostalgic appeal have assured his sustained popularity throughout generations. Older fans who grew up with the original films and cartoons are often anxious to share their enthusiasm for the character with their children or grandkids, carrying the torch from one generation to the next.

Nostalgia is a significant element that contributes to the Pink Panther's continued popularity. The visual style, the character's unique theme music, and the unforgettable antics all evoke nostalgia in fans, which is constantly reignited via repeats, streaming platforms, and the rare new release.

## 9.2 The Panther's Appeal Across Generations.

The Pink Panther's ability to appeal to people of all ages is one of the main reasons the character has survived so long. From youngsters to adults, the series has attracted a large fanbase. This section investigates how, despite changing cultural and entertainment environments, the Pink Panther continues to appeal with various age groups.

## 9.2.1 An Appeal to Children

The Pink Panther provides youngsters with a unique sort of entertainment that is both captivating and easy to grasp. The character's actions are often slapstick, with exaggerated facial expressions, absurd circumstances, and visual comedy that appeal to a younger demographic. The absence of intricate conversation helps youngsters to completely immerse themselves in the action without worrying about comprehending every word stated.

Furthermore, the Pink Panther's style and antics are ageless, making him relatable to children of all ages. Whether it's the classic 1960s cartoons or more modern animated specials and flicks, the Panther's mischievous spirit and colorful personality never fail to delight.

## 9.2.2 The Appeal to Adults.

For adults, Pink Panther combines nostalgia and smart comedy. The original Pink Panther films, notably those featuring Peter Sellers as Inspector Clouseau, were witty and socially conscious, making them suitable for adults. These films' cerebral tone, combined with the Pink Panther's humorous antics, formed an enticing balance for adult audiences.

Furthermore, the character's reputation as a pop cultural icon has solidified his place in the collective memory of adults raised on the series. Many adults have a particular place in their hearts for Pink Panther, whether they recall seeing the film in cinemas or merely hearing the theme song. This sentimental link solidifies the character's place in popular culture, ensuring his relevance throughout generations.

### 9.2.3 The Appeal to Millennials and Generation Z

The Pink Panther has regained importance among younger generations, including Millennials and Generation Z. The character's popularity on social media platforms, particularly via viral videos, memes, and allusions to the Pink Panther theme song, has helped him stay visible. Social media enables a younger audience to connect with the character in ways that earlier generations couldn't, such as sharing video and generating their own memes.

The Pink Panther's capacity to adapt and be reinterpreted in new digital settings keeps him relevant. Whether via internet nostalgia, items suited for current tastes, or reboots such as the 2006 and 2009 films, the Pink Panther continues to captivate and enchant youthful audiences.

# 9.3 Final Thoughts: Legacy and

# Enduring Popularity

The Pink Panther's history is built on its capacity to adapt and stay relevant in a constantly shifting cultural and entertainment world. The Pink Panther has proved to be a flexible and durable presence in popular culture, beginning with a cartoon character and film series and expanding to television, video games, merchandising, and even social media. His impish attitude, refined charisma, and ability to make people laugh without saying a word have guaranteed his popularity throughout decades.

## 9.3.1 Timeless Design and Style.

The Pink Panther's continuing appeal stems from his design. The Panther's sleek, simple body, with his pink color and fine stance, has made him immediately identifiable. His visual simplicity, paired with his sophisticated character, lends him a timeless quality that continues to appeal to viewers.

The refinement of his design enables him to transcend trends and fads, keeping his image new and fascinating.

## 9.3.2 The Continuing Legacy of the Films

The Pink Panther flicks, both the original series starring Peter Sellers and the reboots of the 2000s, have left a lasting impression. The humor, distinctive characters, famous theme song, and general charm of the series continue to inspire future generations of filmmakers, comedians, and fans. The franchise's capacity to persist and grow, whether via reboots or continuous presence in pop culture, assures that the Pink Panther will be relevant for many years to come.

## 9.3.3 Looking Forward: The Future of the Pink Panther

The Pink Panther franchise has a promising future, with additional films, television series, merchandise, and digital material on the way. As entertainment evolves, the Pink Panther will seek new methods to engage viewers. His eternal appeal, global wit, and capacity to adapt to various cultural circumstances assure that he will remain a cherished character for future generations.

Made in United States
Troutdale, OR
04/05/2025